To
Jon
Stephanie
Ben
Sam
Chris
Nicholas

You have truly blessed our lives

Grandmom and Grandpop

Introduction

Becoming a grandparent seemed to sneak up on me. Of course, for many months I had known that my older daughter was pregnant and that I had wanted to become a grandfather. But that hardly prepared me for the event.

I arrived at a client's plant in New Jersey that August morning and the manager's secretary called me to the phone to take the call. I stood by her desk and as I learned the details of that blessed event, tears began to roll down my cheeks. Now six years later, Jon must share his grandpa with a sister and four cousins, but that phone call announcing his birth will always be remembered.

Understand I am certainly no expert on being a grandparent. Some of my friends have as many as ten grandchildren so I am quite a novice as compared to them. Most of their grandchildren live in the same city so my friends have many more hours of experience than I do. Also I can't claim personal experience as a grandchild since I never knew my own grandparents. My children did know and love their four grandparents and I was able to observe some of those special relationships. But I was busy making a career and probably spent too little time observing the delicate and caring interactions between our parents and our children. So this book is being written by a beginner and is for beginners in the wonderful world of grandparenting.

The idea that grandpa should have rules came from Jon. We were playing in his basement a couple of years ago when Jon climbed up on his father's pool table to roll the balls into the pockets. I asked Jon if his father let him get up on the table. He replied: "It's all right if he's not here. That's the rule!" Well, if three-year-old Jon can have his own rules, why shouldn't grandpa have a few rules too?

AN IMPORTANT RULE

There are no rules

Of course, there are rules
of safety:

Don't go into the street.
Don't hit your little sister.
Don't talk back to your mother.
(This is a safety rule that
may prevent a smack on
the child's bottom.)

These rules must be enforced,
even by grandpa.

When it comes to bedtime,
what to eat,
or what to play,
when grandpa's in charge—
there are no rules!

The time with your grandchild
is a very special one.

It is too precious to
have it consumed by
constant referral
to the unwritten rule book.

Part of the enjoyment
your grandchild feels
in being with you
is the realization
that there are no rules.

• • • • •

About babysitting at night—
always read the "just one more" story.
You'll probably learn something from
Dr. Seuss yourself.

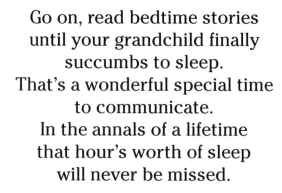

Go on, read bedtime stories
until your grandchild finally
succumbs to sleep.
That's a wonderful special time
to communicate.
In the annals of a lifetime
that hour's worth of sleep
will never be missed.

Admittedly, there is a bit of selfishness
in the "no rules" philosophy.
Grandpa will be remembered for
his fun and tenderness.

• • • • •

Love is best shared
when the rule book is closed
and the warmth of human emotions
can bind together
two generations.

You are engrossed in an
exciting game of Candyland
and you are about to win
when your grandchild says,
"I don't want to play anymore!"
and folds up the board.

Just smile
and wait to be told
what you are going to play next.

You and grandchild
are swinging happily at the park
and it is time to go home for lunch,
but grandchild says, *"No, not yet."*

Absolutely do not invoke the
"Time-for-lunch" rule.
There'll still be something to eat
when you get home.

AN IMPORTANT RULE

Hold the new baby

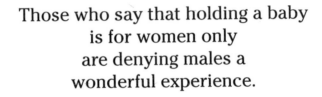

Those who say that holding a baby
is for women only
are denying males a
wonderful experience.

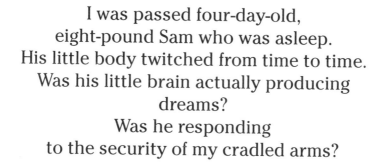

I was passed four-day-old,
eight-pound Sam who was asleep.
His little body twitched from time to time.
Was his little brain actually producing
dreams?
Was he responding
to the security of my cradled arms?

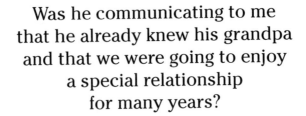

Was he communicating to me
that he already knew his grandpa
and that we were going to enjoy
a special relationship
for many years?

I put my finger in Sam's tiny hand
and felt his fingers actually hold on to me.
Was he saying,
"I know you are there, Grandpa,
and I am glad"?

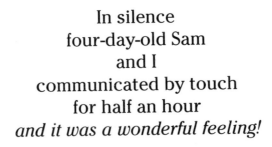

In silence
four-day-old Sam
and I
communicated by touch
for half an hour
and it was a wonderful feeling!

• • • • •

Psychologists will say
Sam and I bonded.

I say: We ***communicated!***

Holding the new baby
is not something you can do
when you find time
several months later.

It is a
once-in-a-lifetime experience
you won't want to miss.

AN IMPORTANT RULE

*The diapers are
for grandma*

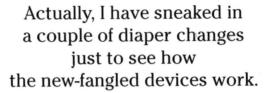

Actually, I have sneaked in
a couple of diaper changes
just to see how
the new-fangled devices work.

● ● ● ● ●

Watch how a grandmother
sweeps up the baby,
sniffs its bottom,
and heads for the changing table.

Grandmothers are bound
to their grandchildren
through the loving act of
diaper-changing
in an even more intimate way
than just holding the baby.

Grandmothers get a special pleasure
from that time alone with the baby
and the feeling of satisfaction
in providing a professional and loving
job of relief.

When baby becomes a toddler
grandmother continues to perform
diaper-changing with professional dignity.

That I admire.

AN IMPORTANT RULE

Be a best friend

Your best friend probably knows the rules
as well as you do,
but is not going to enforce them.

• • • • •

Your best friend is someone you can trust.
Friends do not "tell on you"
or reveal your dreams.

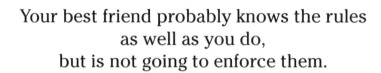

Your best friend is
someone you are comfortable with.
When you are together,
you seem to feel pretty good about yourself.

Now, of course, grandpa will not
replace that kind of friend for a child.
Nor should he.
But for the times the two of you
are together,
"best friend" characteristics
will be rewarding to each.

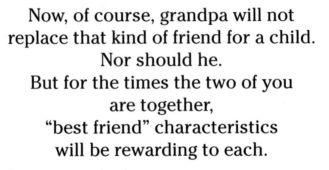

Three-year-old Ben and I
had a wonderful conversation
while he was waiting to fall asleep.
We were best friends.
I glimpsed a smile on his face
as his eyes closed.

Don't select activities
you think "best friends"
should want to do together
without input from your grandchild.

• • • • •

Being a best friend can mean being together
for just a stroll through the woods,
or flying a kite,
or feeding the ducks in the park.

It can be the simplest of activities.

Being a best friend means
listening
as well as talking
and conversing
on the child's level.

• • • • •

Be sure your vocabulary includes words like

proud
good
nice job

Remember that
friendship
is built on
trust.
And sharing little secrets
can strengthen that bond.

The "best friend" relationship
can grow over time.
Someday you'll talk together about
future ambitions
world politics
sports
religion
girlfriends or boyfriends.

The self-esteem
you will have instilled
in your grandchild
may be the greatest gift of all.

Your grandchildren will remember that
when they were with you
they always felt relaxed
and good about themselves.

AN IMPORTANT RULE

Hug a lot

A hug does not require words.

In fact,
there is no word
that can replace
the emotion
of a hug.

When my wife and I meet our grandson
at the end of the jetway
we know he will run toward us
and put his arms up to one of us
to be picked up and hugged.

I always hope it will be me.

(This isn't fair, but carry a surprise
in your pocket
so you know it will be you!)

Where the vocabulary is limited
as with infants
the hug can express
a feeling of tender warmth
between two loving human beings.

• • • • •

Lap-sitting
is a subtle form of hugging.
It provides that tenderness
which more than replaces words.

There will be fewer and fewer opportunities
to hug a grandchild
as the years roll on.

Don't pass up any opportunity to hug.

AN IMPORTANT RULE

Laugh a lot

Other than crying,
smiling is the first emotion
an infant shows with its face.

• • • • •

The first laugh
should be as memorable
as the first word
or the first step
or the first time on the potty.

Because the baby's first laugh
happens so early in life
it likely will go unchronicled.

• • • • •

Communication with a baby
takes place through laughter
long before words have any meaning.

I do not recall any medical caution
against too much laughter
by a baby.

My grandson laughs when I push his swing
so high that his
"tummy is tickling."

My tummy tickles then too.

What makes a grandchild laugh
is not important.
That the child laughs is important.

• • • • •

A little genuine silliness
between grandpa and grandchild
can relieve the stress of the day.

Grandpas are expected to be a little silly
so it is perfectly natural to fill that
important family role.

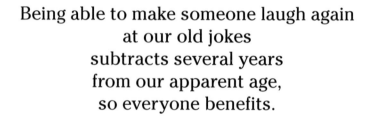

Being able to make someone laugh again
at our old jokes
subtracts several years
from our apparent age,
so everyone benefits.

Laughter is two-way communication
Be sure to laugh at the humor
of your grandchildren.

AN IMPORTANT RULE

Remember who's watching you

Little minds are continually
absorbing and processing observations
with the precision and speed of a
next-generation computer.

IMPORTANT!

Remember the influence you are having
on that grandchild who is watching you.

I am pleased when I am sitting
in the bathroom
and there is a knock on the door
and a little voice says,
"Grandpa, what are you doing?"

• • • • •

I like it when a stool is pulled up next to me
when I am shaving
and a young face studies my every stroke.

It makes me feel good
when a grandchild comes up to me
to watch me "work" at the computer,
even if he has caught me
playing a computer game.

Don't be afraid to
hug and kiss your wife
when the grandchildren are watching.

• • • • •

If grandpa is seen to lose his temper,
it will offset much parental effort
to prevent temper tantrums
from the grandchildren.

The language grandparents use
is soaked up in little minds
as a measure of what is acceptable
or not acceptable to say.

IMPORTANT!

Be sure your grandchildren
do not hear you using
foul language.

Children do look up to grandpa because
he is seen as outside the realm
of direct authority
and therefore someone without bias.

• • • • •

Grandpa's actions will be
considered as
genuine and part of the real world.

AN IMPORTANT RULE

---

*Remember, time
is running out*

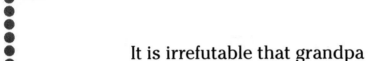

It is irrefutable that grandpa
won't live forever.

• • • • •

Consider that each time
you spend a day with a grandchild,
it may be the last.

Do not put off the potential opportunities
to be with your grandchild.

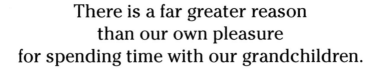

There is a far greater reason
than our own pleasure
for spending time with our grandchildren.

It is the legacy that we wish to leave
with them.

Not spending time with grandchildren
is to miss the opportunity to give them
memories that they may carry with them
throughout their lives.

• • • • •

Secretly, I want to become a
great-grandpa,
although that might be a little greedy!

AN IMPORTANT RULE

Listen!

We all like to be listened to,
and our grandchildren are no exception.

Listening to your grandchildren
can be just as effective
(and certainly cheaper)
as buying them gifts or taking them to an
amusement park.

A young mind understands spoken words
long before it learns how to speak.
That must be *really* frustrating!

Listen carefully to those first
hard-to-understand words
and appreciate
how badly that child wants to communicate.

If you listen intently
and question for understanding,
your grandchild will put more energy into
thinking about what he or she is
going to say.

Listen to a child
because it will make the child feel good.

(Something we all agree is desirable.)

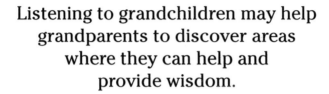

Listening to grandchildren may help
grandparents to discover areas
where they can help and
provide wisdom.

• • • • •

Part of the fun in being with grandchildren
is being able to help them to learn
and listening to them
may give the clue as to what they
want to learn.

Listening helps us not only to become
better grandparents
but also better citizens of a
changing society.

Listen to young grandchildren and you will enjoy listening to older grandchildren's deepest thoughts and dreams—

things that are sometimes difficult to discuss with parents.

At grandpa's house the grandchildren know
not only will they be listened to,
but also what they have to say will be heard.

AN IMPORTANT RULE

*Leave a message
in writing*

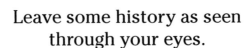

Leave some history as seen
through your eyes.

Do it in writing!

Your grandchildren will someday want to
read your unique story.

Write your story on a computer,
in longhand, or tape-record
your recollections.

• • • • •

You don't have to be anyone special
to have had a life that was exciting
and that will enthrall your grandchildren
if you leave them a glimpse of it.

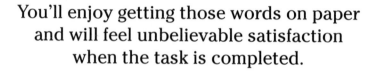

You'll enjoy getting those words on paper
and will feel unbelievable satisfaction
when the task is completed.

And your grandchildren will bless you for
having done that.

Write letters to your grandchildren honoring
special events in their lives.

• • • • •

Write letters to your grandchildren
just to let them know you love them
and are proud of them.

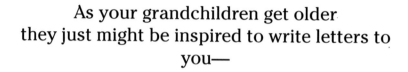

As your grandchildren get older
they just might be inspired to write letters to
you—

good for their education and development,
good for the pleasure they bring you.

Leave some of your wisdom
—fifty or sixty years of it—
for future generations.
Do it in writing!

• • • • •

The birth of a grandchild is a wonderful and
exciting event!
That wonder and excitement continues
throughout life.

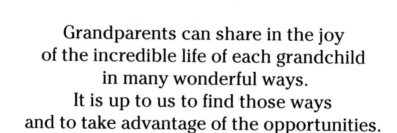

Grandparents can share in the joy
of the incredible life of each grandchild
in many wonderful ways.
It is up to us to find those ways
and to take advantage of the opportunities.

Have fun!
Remember that you will be leaving
precious memories
to those who call you
grandma or grandpa.

These rules come from a
beginner grandpa.
Even more rules are daily unfolding.